JOB
HUNTING

Chris Gillmore FIRP

Published in 2014 by the author
using SilverWood Books Empowered Publishing®

SilverWood Books
30 Queen Charlotte Street, Bristol, BS1 4HJ
www.silverwoodbooks.co.uk

ISBN 978-1-78132-162-1 (paperback)
ISBN 978-1-78132-163-8 (ebook)

British Library Cataloguing in Publication Data
A CIP catalogue record for this book is available from the British Library

Set in Bembo by SilverWood Books
Printed on responsibly sourced paper

Contents

Introduction

The purpose of this booklet is to put forward a practical approach to job hunting, and to give details of other sources of information. I have gathered these resources during my career in the recruitment industry, while working for the employment training provider PTS and as the owner recruitment and employments company Accord Appointments (accordappointments.co.uk).

If you are not used to the business of changing your job, then the prospect of having to do so can be daunting and stressful – particularly if you find yourself thrust into the employment market whether you like it or not.

A successful job search needs to be as well organised as any other responsible task. This means defining the problem through research and analysis, identifying possible courses of action, and deciding which one to take. Progress will need to be reviewed frequently, and thought given to trying alternatives if things are not turning out as planned.

Please note that all names and contact details within this guide have been fictionalized and are for the purpose of illustration only.

Chris Gillmore FIRP
Spring 2014

Job Hunting

1

Job hunting is a skill which few of us have to practice very often and, like any skill which is not used, it can get rusty. But job hunting techniques can be learned and brushed up.

What Can You Offer?

A good start is to analyse your skills and abilities, and list information about yourself. It is worth drawing up a chart similar to the example below: In the left hand column record details of your education and training, employment and leisure activities. Then, against each entry record the information gained by answering the questions printed at the head of the columns. Check that you have included everything. The exercise, if done properly, will take longer than you suppose. The result will be a data bank of information, which can then be drawn upon to extract the information relevant to particular jobs.

Self Assessment	Education and Training	Employment Including company name, industry, product/service	Leisure activities
What did I do?			
What responsibilities?			
What Authority?			
Achievements			
What I enjoyed most and least			

Make sure you recognise every possible asset you can offer a prospective employer.

Often something that looks at first glance like a weakness is in fact a strength. Remember that age means experience and can be a strong selling point with the right employer – while doing a highly specialised job for a long time with the same company may not be a desirable for an employer looking for broad all-round experience, to an employer in the right line of business however, this background may be worth its weight in gold.

Remember your strengths are your selling points.

What Do You Want?

Make list what you want from employer taking the following into consideration:

Job Content
Note the functions you know well and the tasks you are experienced in carrying out.

Status
What level of responsibility are you aiming for? Are you more interested in personal performance or in administration, management, and leadership? Do you want to practice specialism, perhaps to act as a staff advisor or to be a manager with responsibilities?

Salary
    a) What is the minimum you need to cover important or essential aspects of your lifestyle?
    b) What are realistically hoping for?

Location
Discuss with and consider the needs of members of the family who will be effected by any decisions you might make moving home.

Prospects

How ambitious are you? How hard are you prepared to work at furthering your career? (For instance, are you the sort of person who would move home if you are offered promotion, and how good would the offer have to be...)

Look as widely as you are able and be flexible as you can when it comes to – GEOGRAPHICILLY, OCCUPATIONALLY and FINANCIALLY.

Getting Organised

Getting a job can be a full-time work in itself, so you need to be well-organised. Think of the following:

Stationery

Try to use good quality paper and envelopes. Remember even a top quality product gains in appeal when it is well packaged.

Typing

Count on the likelihood that the person who receives your correspondence will be short of time. He/she will assimilate more information if you use a typewriter or word processor for your letters.

Records

You will be surprised at the delays which sometimes occur before you receive a reply or an invitation to interview. Don't expect to rely on your memory – maintain a record along the lines suggested in 'Job Hunting Activities' on page 12.

Time

Set aside time every day, or every other day, and set targets for job leads to be followed up each day or week.

DON'T BE PUT OFF. Most employers may not reply and many will say 'no' but keep trying – applying for over 100 jobs is quite normal.

Job Hunting Activities

Record 1 Advertisement replied to

Date reply sent	
Source of advertisment and date	
Ref No.	
Job Title	
Company	
Date Reply from advertiser received	
Remarks	
Advert and copy of my reply filed at	

Record 2 Approaches to Contacts

Company to contact	
Person to contact and tel no.	
Date letter sent	
Follow up date	
Result	
Proposed date to next contact	
Remarks	
Advert and copy of my reply filed at	

Record 3 Approaches to Agencies

Company to contact	
Person to contact and tel no.	
Date letter sent	
Follow up date	
Result	
Proposed date to next contact	
Remarks	
Advert and copy of my reply filed at	

Researching the Market

The next step is to look at the 'market' to see if it offers opportunities which match what you need, and what you have to offer. Many sources of information are available. (Also see Chapter 8.)

1. Recruitment Advertisements

The list below shows which of the major websites and national newspapers is strongest in vacancies in different specialism. You may also need to scan professional journals and the local press and websites. Find out which days your local paper features appointments and use your local library to look at the professional journals. Below are list of a few job searching links for websites and newspapers.

Websites

> CV Library (www.cv-library.co.uk)
> Jobcentre Plus (https://jobsearch.direct.gov.uk)
> Jobsite (www.jobsite.co.uk)
> Monster (www.monster.co.uk)
> Reed (www.reed.co.uk)
> Total Jobs (www.totaljobs.com)

National Newspapers

> Guardian (guardian.co.uk/media/national-newspapers)
> Telegraph (www.telegraph.co.uk)
> Times (www.thetimes.co.uk/tto/news)
> Examples of local Newspapers
> Echo (www.dailyecho.co.uk)
> The News (www.portsmouth.co.uk)

For a larger source of information where you can find job advertisements see Chapter 8.

2. Employment Agencies/ Consultancies

It may be worth approaching recruitment companies. They charge the employer a fee as a percentage of the salary as introduction fee, and it's worth remembering that recruitment businesses are usually specialists in a particular market and thus maintain a more professional image. Telephone them and ask about the market for your kind of experience. You should at least get some valuable information, and with luck they may even be trying to fill a vacancy that calls for someone like you.

Recruitment companies and agencies are in business to supply people to companies who have slots to fill. You can therefore expect them to be interested in you, if there is a reasonable chance that they can make money from you. You will need to:

- Find the recruitment company/business handling your kind of job.
- Ensure that they have information which tells them what you want, and can offer.

To find appropriate agencies/consultancies you should consult:

- The Recruitment and Employment Confederation Services Website Directory REC Directory (www.rec.uk.com)
- Yellow pages (www.yell.co.uk)
- The Directory of Trainer Support Services (Kogan Pages)

3. Hidden Vacancies
Many vacancies are never advertised and therefore you need to look out for these opportunities, for example – press reports about firms expanding or moving into the area. Many jobs are found through word of mouth, so it is well worth maintaining contact with past colleagues, friends and relatives.

4. Social Media
Most people nowadays use social media sites like LinkedIn, Facebook and Twitter to keep in touch with friends and family, but these tools also can be used for professional networking and job searching.

"Social media gives you a chance to highlight your personality. CV is great for listing skills and experience qualifications. But social media lets you take it beyond that. There might be 100 people qualified for a job, but the employer is looking for someone who is a good fit for the company and team."

Be sure to verify your online reputation by searching your name combined with your city or school or a company you've worked for. Companies may conduct online research about applicants, so if you're posting inappropriate content, chances are high that it will be found, so avoid common mistakes like:

1. Lying or exaggerating your work experience.
2. Sharing sensitive work-related information.
3. Be cautious who you connect with
4. Be careful about what photos you share.

Complete a LinkedIn profile as many recruiters and companies search LinkedIn for candidates. This is one place to put your best foot forward and attract employers. Don't treat it as an online resume with every career detail – just include highlights of your work history and accomplishments. (See Chapter 8 for list of social media sites.)

Applying for Jobs

2

How to Get an Interview

You will become aware that there are different avenues which lead to interviews, and different techniques should be employed if you are to have the success you should expect. They are:

- replying to recruitment advertisements
- making use of people you know
- researching companies who have not advertised their needs
- using recruitment and employment Business

Recruitment Advertisements

When you see an advertisement which describes just the job you are looking for resist the natural reaction to send a photocopy of your CV under cover of a letter which adds very little to the information offered. Your aim is to be shortlisted and subsequently interviewed.

Analyse the job. Look carefully at the information given regarding:

Job functions	Personal qualities
Responsibilities	Interest
Training prospects	Personality
Conditions of employment	Ambitions
Type of person sought after	
Qualifications	

List what you consider to be the recruiter's main needs and write your covering letter highlighting these needs, saying briefly how you satisfy each need and, if appropriate, and drawing attention to that part of your CV which provides the supporting evidence – **Be positive.**

Example of an Advert

WORKS MANAGER

c£20,000pa ⎯⎯⎯⎯⎯⎯⎯⎯⎯⎯ Dorset

Phillips Ltd, a leading manufacturer of cultivation machines for the agricultural industry, employs 500 people in a new, purpose-built factory situated in the heart of Dorset.

A Works Manager is sought to be responsible to the MD for planning and achieving production to agreed schedules. Production workers, predominantly male and numbering approximately 380 are engaged in traditional machining, fabrication assembly and finishing operations. Applicants must have a record of successful production management in engineering with sufficient practical knowledge, to understand and adopt improved manufacturing methods. Also they must demonstrate an ability to preserve harmonious working relations.

Minimum Qualification HNC
Salary negotiable c£20,000 + car, assistance with relocation
CV to Mr. J Clark Personnel Manager
Phillips Ltd, Penstone Street
Antwich, Dorset, AN1 3QP   REF: 73/127

If the advertisement from a company employing 400 production operators engaged in making cultivation machines for agriculture applications and the needs are for someone with:

- Experience of production management with union environments

- Well-developed skills in preserving harmonious work relations
- At least HNC

Example of a Covering Letter

FAO Mr J Clark
Personnel Manager

Phillips Ltd
Penstone Street
Antwich, Dorset
AN1 3QP

R L Gillmore
2 Stubbington
Portsmouth
PO2 2NL

01705 668705

20 December 2014
Reference: 73/127 Works Manager

Dear Mr Clark,

I refer to your advertisement for the above vacancy. I believe that my experience matches your requirements:

Production Manager
I have had control of 300 production workers in an environment identical to yours.

Engineering Knowledge
Gained by progression from toolmaker, through drawing office, and work study. Machining, fabrication and finishing processes were identical to yours.

Industrial Relations
You will see from my CV that I have been responsible for, and successful in, improving and maintaining good relations in my previous employment.

BSc Passed in 1973. My CV gives all other qualifications.

I look forward to hearing from you.

Yours sincerely,
Mr R L Gillmore

Writing a Curriculum Vitae

3

To accompany your covering letter you will need to prepare a CV which contains the information needed to substantiate your claim to the recruiter. A good CV is an essential tool when looking for work. It is therefore worth spending time on getting it right.

You want your CV to make a good impression. This means presenting the facts about you in a clear and positive light. The chart you have already drawn up about yourself (self-assessment) should provide you with all the information you need for your CV. These headings are useful:

- Name
- Address
- Phone Number
- Email Address
- Date of Birth
- General Health
- Qualifications
- Training
- Career history
- Driving License
- Spare-time activities
- Additional information

It is usual to present the latest information first unless an employer requests otherwise. What you have done recently will be of more interest to a prospective employer. See the following sample for an example of a completed CV.

A CV doesn't have to be a 'once and for all' thing. It should evolve as you learn new skills or do new things – add them to your CV. It is worthwhile keeping your CV up-to-date regularly.

CURRICULUM VITAE

Robert Lewis Gillmore
2 Stubbington, Portsmouth, Hampshire, PO2 2NL

Tel: Portsmouth (01705) 668705 **email:** kak@accordappointments.com

QUALIFICATIONS

1970-73	BSc (Mech Eng) Class 11.1 – Leeds University
1966-70	5 GCE 'O' levels; 3 'A' levels – Chemistry (B), Physics (B), Mathematics (C)

Professional	Member of the Institute of Mechanical Engineers
	CSCS Card Holder
	Digital Tacho Card

TRAINING

1988 onwards — External management training course including effective time management. This assisted me in organising the office more efficiently and sharpened my administrative skills.

AJAX Ltd in-house personnel recruitment training course. Provided me with a basic appreciation of the recruitment process.

CAREER HISTORY

Nov 1989-Present — AJAX Ltd (Mowing Machine Manufacturers)
Works Manager
Responsible for all production, warehousing and distribution for home and overseas orders

Forecasting, planning and achievement of output, capital purchasing decisions. Industrial relations.

ADDITIONAL INFORMATION

Date of Birth	1 April 1950
General health	Excellent
Driving license	Full clean car and 7.5 Ton driving license with valid Digital Card

REFERENCES

Both Personal and Employers references supplied on request

References

These are not essential in the initial CV, but it is worth having a record of both personal and business referees ready for when you are shortlisted for or successful at an interview. You should also make sure that the referee is informed that he/she may be approached for a reference.

Your CV Should Be:

- Neat – the best standard you can achieve in content and layout - it should be typed.
- Short – two sides of a sheet of A4 paper should normally be enough. Long CVs may be put aside and not fully considered. Tailor your CV towards each advertised job where possible (the average recruiter will spend 30 Seconds looking at a CV).
- Positive – do more than just giving a list of responsibilities from your present and previous job descriptions. Highlight your achievements, strengths, successes and contributions, quantify facts where you can, and remember you are selling yourself. Use positive/action words where you can. Some examples are given below:

Achieved	Efficient	Productive
Administered	Engineered	Proficient
Analysed	Established	Profitable
Built	Expanded	Qualified
Capable	Experienced	Repaired
Competent	Guided	Resourceful
Communicated	Implemented	Sold
Consistent	Improved	Specialised
Controlled	Initiated	Stable
Co-ordinated	Led	Successful
Created	Managed	Supervised
Designed	Monitored	Trained
Developed	Organised	Versatile
Directed	Participated	Wide background
Economical	Positive	
Effective	Processed	

CV Myths

- **Age and date of births on a CV** – In my view most employers seek the right person to do the job no matter the age.
- **Lying on your CV** – In many cases an employer can tell early on about lies, especially if you are applying for similar position within a similar organisation. Lies always have a way of coming out and biting you on the backside.

Use Your CV

A CV provides you with a useful summary about yourself. You can use it:

- As the main part of your application for a job which asks for a CV.
- When you are asked to apply in writing.
- Information to help you when you fill in application forms.
- To jog your memory when you phone employers.
- When you visit possible employers.
- A reminder for yourself when you prepare for interviews.

Example of a Letter of Application Accomanying a CV

R L Gillmore
2 Stubbington
Portsmouth
PO2 2NL

01705 668705

FAO Mr D F Thomson
BG (Plastics) Ltd
Healey Park Industrial Estate
Ralston
Durbridge
DU5 7TL

17 April 2014

Dear Mr Thomson,

I am writing to apply for the position of Warehouse Person advertised in the Evening News on the 17 April 2014.

Please find enclosed a copy of my Curriculum Vitae. My Career Summary indicates that I have worked within fully computerised, and manual warehousing environments for over eight years. With these achievements to date coupled with a valid fork lift operators certificate, I can offer this position full potential.

I am looking forward to hearing from you in the near future, however, if you require any further information please do not hesitate to contact me.

Yours sincerely,
Mr R L Gillmore

Application Forms | 4

Employers often require an application form to be completed instead of a letter of application or CV. As they are used to decide who should be invited to interview, it is important to pay careful attention to their completion. If you complete the application form in by hand, use clear block capitals. You should answer each question fully, and don't leave any box blank – to do so can give an impression of carelessness.

Most application forms ask fairly standard factual questions, but an increasing number require the applicant to explain what qualities/ skills they have which makes them suitable for the job. This is an opportunity for you to market yourself to the employer. Using the information from your skills chart and/or CV state precisely how your experiences, skills and personal qualities match the needs of the employer. **Be positive** – do more than just giving a list of responsibilities from your previous job descriptions. Emphasize your achievements, strengths, successes and contributions, and quantify where you can.

Sending in Your Application

Make sure you send in your application promptly, and clearly addressed to the right person. It is not usual to include a self-addressed envelope unless asked for, and it is recommended that you do not fax your application unless invited to do so.

Application Form Positive Key Words:

- Team working
- Interactive exercise & tips for group work exercises in selection centres
- Making effective presentations
- Action planning
- Techniques to reach your goals
- Decision making skills
- Problem-solving skills
- Time management
- Commercial awareness
- Spoken communication
- Written communication
- Persuading, influencing and negotiating skills
- Leadership skills including a leadership styles exercise
- Language skills
- Computing skills
- Numeracy
- Striving for excellence
- Determination
- Adaptability
- Assertiveness
- Lateral thinking

Application Form Techniques:

Ten point plan to make a good impression

1 Make a couple of copies of the application form.

2 Read through the application form fully.

3 Make notes on the photocopied application form as you read through.

4 Answer every question fully, even if you have to write 'None', 'Not Applicable'.

5 Use your CV to help you detail your experience.

6 On a clean copy of your application form, complete each question fully from your notes made on whilst reading through the application form.

7 Use black pen in BLOCK LETTERS when writing your application form unless instructed otherwise.

8 After completing the draft copy of your application form, get a friend or family member to proofread it for you.

9 Where possible use correct grammar and correct phrasing.

10 Remember! This is your sales pitch to get them to invite you into an interview. Keep a copy.

Questions you may be asked:
- Employment History of the last five years
- Job title and duties
- Qualifications
- Education
- Past time and sporting activities
- Skills you offer the position
- Strengths and weaknesses

Example of a Letter Requesting Application Form

FAO Mr D F Thomson
BG (Plastics) Ltd
Healey Park Industrial Estate
Ralston
Durbridge
DU5 7TL

R L Gillmore
2 Stubbington
Portsmouth
PO2 2NL
01705 668705

17 April 2014
Reference: Vacancy for a Van Driver XL/2243

Dear Mr Thomson,

Could you please forward me an application form for the vacancy for a van driver advertised in the Evening News on 17 April 2014.

I look forward to hearing from you in the near future.

Yours sincerely,
Mr R L Gillmore

Speculative Approach 5

There are a number of advantages in writing to a potential employer speculatively, and creating your own opportunity or finding hidden vacancies. You will be displaying initiative and resourcefulness, and if your curriculum vitae lands on a potential employers desk before he spends money advertising or sourcing the vacancy out to a recruitment company you may be considered on your own without any competition. Occasionally an employer may create a special opening for the right candidate.

- Write to the companies you think will be most likely to have an opening for someone with your track record.
- Send out your letters and career summaries/CV in small batches. Make sure each one is typed, looks short, and is addressed to the individual to whom you would report if you were to join that company.
- Ensure that you retain control by making it clear in the letter that you will telephone for their reaction to your letter.

Keep a record of the contacts you make – an employer may get back to you some time later. (See 'Job Hunting Activities' on page 12).

Speculative approaches by telephone and personal visits to firms can also be successful ways of making contact. It will usually be necessary to be bold and persistent. It is, important that you manage to speak to the right person, so try to find out in advance who is responsible for recruitment and ask for them by name. If telephoning, ask for an interview to discuss openings, and ask if you can send a CV in case any unexpected vacancies arise. On visits don't be put off if there are no current vacancies – leave your CV. They may also be able to suggest other contacts you could try, but if not ask.

Making Use of People You Know

Friends, relatives and other people you know may be well placed to hear of actual or impending opportunities. Former business contacts can be particularly valuable. Provided you equip them to do so they can become your advocates. Let them know you are looking and:

- Send them a copy of your CV.
- Tell them your requirements in terms of salary, level of responsibility and geographical location.
- Remind them from time to time that you are still looking for work.

Make a list of people, agencies it may be worth contacting and work through systematically, and keep a record (see 'Job Hunting Activities' on page 12) to help keep in touch with the right people.

Example of a Speculative Approach

The Personnel Manager
Jenkinson Engineering PLC
Washington St
West Bridgeford
Nottingham, NG8 5PS
DU5 7TL

R L Gillmore
2 Stubbington
Portsmouth
PO2 2NL
01705 668705

20 November 2014

Dear Sir/Madam,

I read a report in the *Nottingham Evening Post* of 18 November that your company has recently received several large export orders, and that you are planning an expansion. In anticipation of: the need for new staff I am writing in the hope that there may be an opening for someone with my background.

I have several years' experience as works manager in the engineering field, and I enclose a copy of my CV for your consideration should a suitable vacancy arise.

May I come and talk to you about possible opportunities I will telephone you on 25 November to make an appointment.

Yours sincerely,
Mr R L Gillmore

Example of a Speculative Approach

17 April 2014

Dear Mr Thomson,

I am writing to you reference the possibility of any vacancies that you may have, that could fit the variety of skills I can offer you within your company.

Please find enclosed a copy of my Curriculum Vitae. My Career Summary indicates that I have worked within fully computerised, and manual warehousing environements for over eight years, and with these achievements to date coupled with a valid fork lift operators certificate, I can offer this position full potential.

I will telephone you in the following weeks, but please do not hesitate to contact me if you require any further information and I look forward to hearing from you in the near future.

Yours sincerely,
Mr R L Gillmore

Interview 6

Your contacts with potential employers should hopefully result in invitations to interview, though don't expect to get an interview every time. At this stage employers are seriously interested in you, because on paper your experience and achievements have given them some hope that you might satisfy their requirements. This is the point at which you have the opportunity to 'prove yourself'.

First of all, it is important to remember the purpose of the interview. It provides the employer with an opportunity to judge your suitability for the job and assess you in relation to the other candidates applying for the position within their company.

It is also your chance to find out more about the job. You can discuss it with the employer, meet other people in the organisation, look at the establishment, find out more about the product or service and its market, and discuss training and career prospects within the company.

Large employers often use additional selection techniques to supplement the interview. These may include intelligence tests, critical thinking and other aptitude tests, personal preference questionnaires, group discussions, and group or individual exercises or presentations to see how well you can cope with particular problems. If such methods are used they are certain to be explained clearly before you start. You are also likely to be asked to assess how well you think you have done, so think about this in advance.

Preparing for an Interview

1. Confirm you will attend and if appropriate ask about any reimbursement of expenses which will be incurred i.e. for second interview etc.

2. Plan your journey and always have an alternative to the chosen method of travel.

3. Research, the company's products/services. A phone call will usually produce reports and sales literature. Also look their details up in the directories listed in Chapter 8 Source of Information.

4. Decide what you will take with you e.g. CV and job specification.

5. Make notes of any points you may wish to clear. A checklist of subjects to prepare questions on could include:
   - Product and services.
   - Locations, organisation or size.
   - Chief duties.
   - Responsibilities – to whom? for what? for whom?
   - Career development and training opportunities.

6. You should also prepare for questions. Those most commonly encountered include:
   - Where does your main experience lay?
   - What were the main responsibilities in your last job?
   - What were the main problem areas in the job?
   - What do you do particularly well?
   - What are your career objectives?
   - Why did you leave your last job?
   - Why do you want to join this organisation?
   - What appeals to you about the job for which you are applying?
   - Are there any people you find difficulty working with?
   - What do you want to be doing in five years time?
   - What are your strong points?
   - What are your weak points?
   - Why should we employ you?

Also don't be surprised by the awkward or unusual question. If one arises keep calm as these questions are usually aimed to test you under pressure. Practice questions and answers with a friend or relative to help increase your self-confidence.

7. Decide what to wear. Generally go for formality: interviewers often expect a more 'dressed' appearance then they themselves adopt.

8. Establish the interviewer's position as this will influence the way you approach your meeting. A personnel officer assessing candidates for a short list will not usually be in a position to discuss technicalities; and the sales manager is unlikely to be able to give you details of the company pension schemes. However, occasionally, personnel staff are equipped with lists of technical question and trained to assess your responses even though they are not experts themselves. Remember it is not unusual to be interviewed by more than one person.

9. Use every opportunity to stress that you are not just after any old job but that you are genuinely keen to work for the company that is interviewing you. Turn any perceived negatives into positives.

10. Sometimes employers may ask for applicants to give a presentation on a given subject. Prepare well and practice; in particular ensure you have the timing right and you keep your presentation relevant.

Above all, try not to treat the interview as an examination in which you are always on the receiving end. Use it as an opportunity for an exchange of information. Do not be afraid to ask for more information or to ask your own questions.

At the Interview

At the interview be as natural as possible. There are a number of points that are worth bearing in mind:

- Do not sit until invited – or until the interviewer sits.
- Do not criticise your past employers.
- Do not swear – even mildly.
- Do not interrupt.
- Do not 'interview' the interviewer, even if his/her technique is terrible.
- Do not argue. If it becomes clear that your views differ from the interviewer's move on to safer ground.
- Do not be personal or familiar.
- Do not constantly repeat questions – very few parrots make it to the boardroom.
- Do not ask about salary; always try encouraging the other side to open the bidding.
- Do not draw attention to any of your weaknesses (physical shortcomings, lack of qualifications, long time out of work) by making apologies or constant reference to it, and if any come up then turn negatives into positives wherever possible.
- Do look at the interviewer and use his/her name at least once.
- Do smile – smiling is in, but laughing is out. There's a very thin line dividing between joviality and sarcasm.
- Watch out for any distracting mannerisms you may have such as repeatedly crossing and uncrossing your legs.
- Do tell the truth.
- Do offer to leave the room if the interviewer receives a phone call (most interviewers will stop incoming calls).
- If the interviewer has omitted to cover a subject which you think is important and it's in your favour, make sure you include it. You may be asked at the end of the interview if you have any questions. If not, say 'May I just say one thing...?'

Also remember during discussions (and in your letters) employers look again at people who can:

- Cut costs
- Maintain competitive advantage
- Make it look better
- Improve the packaging
- Get it done more quickly
- Avoid potential problems
- Improve appearance
- Organise
- Increase sales/profits/turnover
- Expedite the workflow
- Make the boss look good
- Use old things in a new way
- Provide more information
- Cut down time
- Open more territories
- Provide a tax advantage
- Reduce the risks
- Meet deadlines easily
- Cut staff costs
- Reduce inventories
- Develop staff performance
- Turn round a bad situation
- Introduce new systems
- Improve teamwork and relationships

Finally, remember that the interviewer is hoping that you will have the experience and qualities which are sought.

The most important information you can offer is that which shows you have already successfully carried out the duties and responsibilities at issue.

After the interview, and while it is fresh in your mind, decide how you think it went. Note any questions that you found difficult or were unprepared for. Learn from each interview and aim to become more confident and knowledgeable.

If you subsequently find out that you have been unsuccessful, phone the employer and try to find out why. You can say that you respect the decision, but would appreciate some feedback to help you with future job applications. You will not always get a straight answer, but when you do, it may well highlight a weakness of which you were not aware or confirm one you suspected. Armed with this knowledge you can then take whatever remedial action is appropriate.

Interview Techniques 1:

Ten point plan to make a good impression

1   Be pleasant and polite from the start.

2   Knock first.

3   Don't sit down until you are offered to.

4   No smoking.

5   Don't be a sloucher. Just relax in a comfortable upright position.

6   Be confident.

7   Don't be flippant. Try and be on the same wavelength as the interviewer.

8   What qualities are they looking for?

9   Make sure you know the name of the interviewer.

10   Remember! The interviewer is looking for someone who's going to put a lot into the job ability with enthusiasm.

Questions you may be asked:

- Why do you want this job?
- Tell me about yourself...
- What makes you think you would be good at this job?
- What do you do in your spare time?
- What qualities do you think you have to offer?
- What is your ultimate admissions?

Interview Techniques 2:

Be prepared

Important points you may want to raise

The interviewer will properly explain most details about the job. But you will have your own questions to ask.

Do your homework. Show genuine interest in the job and the company you applied for.

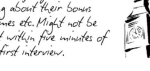

Don't appear too eager. Wait until the interviewer asks... and that is your opportunity.

Use your judgement when asking about their bonus schemes etc. Might not be right within five minutes of the first interview.

✓ Hair
✓ Teeth
✓ Nails
✓ Clothes
✓ Shoes

Use your common sense about appearance, ensuring you look the part.

Hours
• What are the normal working hours?
• Are there any unusual hours?

Pay
• Will I be paid overtime?
• What is the pay?
• How often is it reviewed?
• Will I be paid monthly or weekly?

Holiday

• What about holiday arrangements?

People
• With whom will I be working?
• To whom will I be directly responsible?

Career

• What are the promotional possibilities?
• What training will be given?
• When may I expect a decision?
• When would I be expected to start?

And finally:

The night before the interview you need to ask yourself:
• Exactly where am I going?
• How am I going to get there?
• Who am I going to see?
• What time is the appointment?

Good luck!

Review

7

Regularly review your own personal job hunting program. Re-examine some of the questions you answered when you first thought about embarking upon the next stage of your career or job search. The points to look at are represented below.

Personal Questionnaire

1. How long have I been actively job seeking?
2. What sources am I using to identify suitable vacancies?
   □ National Press & Local Press
   □ Specialist Journals
   □ Other/List of advertise jobs
   □ Employment & Recruitment Company
   □ Own Contacts
3. What sort of job am I seeking?
4. How many job applications have I made?
5. How many interviews have I attended?
6. How many job offers have I had (where applicable) and reasons for not accepting them?
7. At what stage do most often fail?
   • At the short list stage:
      Have I researched the company?
      Was my application relevant?
      Am I aiming for the right market/position or level of job?

- At the interview stage:
  Do I have a weakness in technique?
  Was I well enough prepared?
  Was I too vague/arrogant/unassertive/aggressive?

Do I Need to Review My Job Requirements?

8. How far do my own qualifications and experience match the job opportunities available?
9. What other jobs can I realistically consider? List them.
10. What up-to-date skills do I need for these jobs? What skills/updating can I acquire by training?
11. Do I need to consider a career change? And if so, have I a clear idea of what I intend to do and my prospects in the job market? If not, what information/advice should I seek?
12. What salary do I have in mind as a minimum negotiating figure?
13. In which areas could I work without moving home?
14. Have I considered moving home: if so, where?
15. Have I considered self-employment/setting up in business?
16. When did I last review the information and presentation of my career history used for job applications?

Source of Information

8

Information on Companies

Market research will probably play a major part in your job hunting action plan. The list of sources given below is not comprehensive – you may well be able to add to it – but it will form a useful starting point. Most of the reference works will be available in a nearby library, and because organisations are subject to change you should always consult the most up-to-date directory possible.

Below is a small list of where to find information on companies. The information sources are not specifically careers-related, but may be useful if you are looking for information on a company which is not a regular recruiter, or you want to make speculative applications to companies in a specific business or geographical area.

- **Companies House** (www.companieshouse.gov.uk) allows you to get name, address and brief details of all registered UK companies.
- **Dun & Bradstreet** (www.dnb.co.uk) the world's most comprehensive global business database, with information on over 210 million companies that's updated regularly.
- **Share Cast** (www.sharecast.com) is a database of newspaper articles on companies that may be expanding and recruiting for staff.

- **Financial Times** (www.annualreports.ft.com) free service providing access to annual reports and other company information.
- **Yellow Pages** (www.yell.com) Yellow Pages on the web.
- **BBC News Business Section** (news.bbc.co.uk) is a good place to find the latest business news and economic data. There is also a search section where you can find articles about particular companies.
- **British Services** (www.britishservices.co.uk) is a comprehensive resource covering major governing bodies, government departments, associations and resources of over 100 industries in the UK along with non-profit organisations, charities, groups, clubs and businesses, and has broad list of trade associations and regulatory bodies (www.britishservices.co.uk/associations.htm).
- **Directory of UK Organisations** (www.dotukdirectory.co.uk)
- **Scoot** (www.scoot.co.uk) is an online business directory with information about suppliers of products and services in the UK.
- **Kelly's Business Directory** provides background information on all major firms (products, growth, number of employees).
- **UK Kompass Register** is published annually in two volumes: one of which lists companies and gives basic facts on location, activities, staffing, directors etc.

Books about Job Hunting Techniques

There are many books about coping with redundancy and job hunting. A number are listed below. They can be obtained from public libraries and bookshops.

Getting that Job by Anthony Brown Book Guild
Changing Your Job by Godfrey Golzen & Philip Plumbley
Great Answers to Tough Interview Questions by Martin Yate
The Daily Telegraph Recruitment Handbook
How to be interviewed by D Mackenzie Davey & P McDonnell
Guidelines for the Redundant Manager by SD Webb
Working for Yourself by Jonathon Reuvid
What Colour is Your Parachute by Richard Bolles
How to Write a Curriculum Vitae by University of London Careers
Job Hunting for Women by Margaret Wallis
Advisory Service (ULCAS)
British Institute of Management workbook series
Godfrey Golzen Penguin Business series

Useful Numbers

ACAS	0845 747 4747
Attendance Allowance	0845 712 3456
Disability Living Allowance (Textphone)	0845 722 4433
National Insurance Number	0845 600 0643
National Insurance Registrations Helpline	0300 200 3502
(Textphone)	0845 915 3296
Bereavement Benefit	0845 608 8601
Carers Allowance	0845 608 4321
Child Benefits	0300 200 3100
(Textphone)	0300 200 3103
Employers Direct	0845 601 2001
(Textphone)	0845 601 2001
Incapacity Benefits	0845 479 5127
Income Support	0843 515 9418
Inland Revenue (Employees)	0845 300 0627
Inland Revenue (Employers)	0300 200 3200
Jobseekers Direct 24/7	0843 479 5556
Jobseekers Allowance	0843 479 5234
Jobcentre Plus Contact Centre	0800 055 6688
Maternity Allowance	0800 055 6688/0845 6088 610
Pension Centre – enquiries	0845 606 0265
(Textphone)	0845 606 0285
Pension Credit – claims	0800 731 7898
(Textphone)	0800 731 7339
Tax Credits	0845 300 3900
(Textphone)	0845 300 3909
Sure Start Maternity	0845 608 8580

* Numbers were correct at time of print.

Recruitment Website Advertisements

Accjobs   www.accjobs.com
UK based Accounting, Banking and Finance job board, containing jobs for accountants, banking, and financial professionals.

Agency Central   www.agencycentral.co.uk
Quickly find the most suitable recruitment agencies for your needs, using our unique Recruitment Agency Directory

All Jobs UK   www.alljobsuk.com
Browse alljobsuk.com for recruitment agencies, major employers, recruiters and for online recruitment index.

Career Builder   www.careerbuilder.co.uk
Careerbuilder unique job matching technology recommends jobs that are personalised for you. Personalised jobs by targeting jobs that match keywords in your CV, the jobs you view and ultimately the jobs you apply for. The more you use CareerBuilder.co.uk the better the job matches become.

Careers and Jobs UK   www.careersandjobsuk.com
Careers and Jobs UK contains one of the largest selections of temporary and permanent UK jobs from top employers and recruitment agencies but makes it really easy for you to drill down to the job that you want.

Caterer   www.caterer.com
Catering jobs, hotel jobs, chef jobs, hospitality jobs, pub management jobs, bar jobs.

Click a job www.clickajob.co.uk
Every day it serves thousands of jobseekers across the entire job market, finding and offering them the best jobs in the country, wherever they've been posted on the Internet.

City Jobs www.cityjobs.com
City Jobs is the UK's leading job site in Banking, Finance, Accountancy, Insurance, and Legal. 1000's of jobs from the UK's top recruitment agencies.

Engineering Jobs www.engineeringjobs.co.uk
No need to register for e.ngineering jobs with links to recruitment agency and employer websites. Engineering jobs in the following sectors: civil, structural, mechanical, electrical, chemical, software, aerospace, automotive, utilities engineering and pharmaceutical engineering.

eFinancial Careers www.efinancialcareers.co.uk
Find a New Career in Finance & IT. Search, Upload CV and Apply.

Eteach www.eteach.com
Eteach is the leading education jobsite; search teaching jobs, support staff jobs and all the latest jobs in education. Great teaching jobs in London, Birmingham and more.

Euro Jobs www.eurojobs.com
Search the euro job directory.

Fish4 www.fish4.co.uk
UK's best jobs site. Work wanted, apply for jobs online. New vacancies daily, recruitment agents. Job adverts, finding staff in London and UK.

Gis-a-Job www.gis-jobs.co.uk
The one stop shop for all your GIS recruitment advertising and job searching needs.

Insurance Jobs Board   www.insurancejobsboard.com

Insurance jobs, insurance recruitment and financial Services jobs portal for the UK. 1000's of insurance jobs and financial jobs.

Inretail   www.inretail.co.uk

Search 1000's of retail jobs with the leading retail job finder.

Guardian Jobs   www.jobs.guardian.co.uk

Find your perfect job on Guardian Jobs. Apply for jobs in the public sector, education jobs, media jobs, graduate jobs and government jobs available today.

Jobseekers Direct   jobseekers.direct.gov.uk

The Jobcentre Plus online job search. Search and apply for jobs, voluntary work and childcare provision anywhere in the UK.

The Sun Jobs   jobs.thesun.co.uk/home/home.aspx

Everyday this job site will be updated with fab new jobs with hundreds of vacancies in every sector.

Jobsite   www.jobsite.co.uk

Jobsite is a leading UK online recruitment site, dedicated to helping you find your next job. We're not a recruitment agency ourselves, but lots of agencies and employers use our website every day, to find people just like you.

Job Serve   www.jobserve.com

The largest UK jobsite, with plenty of IT jobs and sub-sites for other sectors. A large variety of agencies use this service.

JobSearch   www.jobsearch.co.uk

JobSearch advertises jobs in all sectors including IT, Sales, Marketing, Secretarial & Admin, Legal, Engineering and Finance. As part of Trinity Mirror Digital Recruitment, the UK's largest portfolio of specialist market-leading jobsites, it attracts candidates across a range of industry verticals including TotallyLegal (lawyers), PlanetRecruit (IT professionals), The Career Engineer, SecsintheCity (secretaries) and GAAPweb (accountancy and finance professionals).

Leisure Vacancies   www.leisurevacancies.co.uk
Leisure Vacancies Site. Jobs from entry to senior management. leisure jobs, retail, hotel, golf, sport, fitness, bar, events, retail, careers, restaurant, spa, cruise and travel.

London Jobs   www.londonjobs.co.uk
Search the latest job vacancies in London.

Monster   www.monster.co.uk
Find the job that's right for you. Use Monster's resources to create a killer CV, search for jobs, prepare for interviews, and launch your career.

Red Gold Fish   www.redgoldfish.co.uk
This job Search facility provides access to UK jobs online. Search for the latest job vacancies today or register.

Reed   www.reed.co.uk
Find your next job on the UK's number one job site. Search and apply for jobs online, prepare for an interview, recruit staff and start your career.

Retail Moves   www.retailmoves.com
Retail jobs – vacancies, and recruitment.

Sales Target   www.caterer.com
Sales recruitment jobsite for sales professionals. Find 1000s of UK sales jobs across all sales sectors.

Simply Sales Jobs   www.simplysalesjobs.co.uk
Search 1000s of sales jobs including telesales,, sales manager jobs and sales assistant jobs from the UKs leading sales recruiters and companies.

Simply Marketing Jobs   www.simplymarketingjobs.co.uk
Search 1000s of Marketing jobs including marketing assistant jobs, marketing jobs London, advertising jobs and marketing PR jobs.

Total Jobs   www.totaljobs.com
Start your job search on totaljobs.com, the UK's largest job site. With thousands of new vacancies added daily, you're sure to find a job that's right for you.

Top Jobs   www.tiptopjob.com
International tip top job site. This is the online recruitment service for jobseekers to search jobs and recruiters to advertise jobs and vacancies in the UK and worldwide. Search and find a job today!

Workthing   www.workthing.com
Workthing exclusively advertises job vacancies direct from employers, covering jobs in all sectors and at all levels. Popular job categories include: sales and marketing, IT, customer service and graduate. The site offers job seeker a variety of ways to target the right employer from searching job postings and adding your CV to a database for potential employers to browse.

Planet Recruit   www.planetrecruit.com
Lists a large number of jobs and posts CVs to job agencies and displays jobs from other hot online jobsites, including workthing.com

Social Media

Social media networking has been around for an age now. It's the simple act of expanding the number of people you know by meeting your friends' friends, their friends' friends and so on. In fact, many of us today use LinkedIn, Twitter and Facebook to promote our existing and upcoming businesses. And people looking to connect with other business-associated contacts usually move to sites like LinkedIn, but one needs to understand that social media is beyond Twitter, Facebook, LinkedIn and Blogs. Below is a list of few social media sites that might be of interest:

1. **Facebook**: To access Facebook you must create an account on the site which is free. Facebook's terms of use state that members must be at least 13 years old with valid email ID's. After updating you're details, your Facebook profile is generated. Using Facebook. com you can search companies profiles and gain insight in to potential employers or vacancies.

2. **MySpace**: On Myspace, your social network starts growing from the first day. When you join Myspace, the first step is to create a profile. You then, invite friends to join there and search for your friends on already profiled on Myspace these friends become your initial Friend Space. Once the friendship is confirmed all the people in your friends' Friend Space become part of your network. In that sense, everyone on Myspace is in your Extended Network. As part of terms of Myspace, the user must be at least 14 years old to register.

3. **Twitter**: Twitter is a very simple service that is rapidly becoming one of the most talked-about social

networking service providers. When you have a Twitter account, you can use the service to post and receive messages to a network of contacts, as opposed to send bulk email messages. You can build your network of contacts, and invite others to receive your Tweets, and can follow other members' posts. Twitter makes it easy to opt into or out of networks. Additionally, you can choose to stop following a specific person's feed.

4. **LinkedIn**: LinkedIn is an online social network for business professionals, which is designed specifically for professional networking, to help them find a job, discover sales leads, connect with potential business partners. Unlike most of the other social networks, LinkedIn does not focus on making friends or sharing media like photos, videos and music. To start using LinkedIn you need to register and create a profile page. To register to LinkedIn, you need to provide personal information. You can update the profile with your education and job details and a summary. Additionally, you can also give and receive recommendations from co-workers and bosses. There are more than 75 million professionals registered on LinkedIn.

5. **Bebo**: In the United Kingdom, Bebo is a social network that allows users to create social networking profiles for free. It offers many of the same features as other social networking sites. You can register a free account with Bebo and upload photos, videos and information. The site lets you connect with old friends and make new ones using a unique user interface. The site boasts users from more than a dozen countries, including the United States, Australia, Canada, Poland, France and Germany.

6. **Friendster**: Friendster was designed as a place to connect with friends, family, colleagues and new friends over the Internet. However, it went beyond just a one-way communication. Using Friendster, you

can connect with friends and family, meet new people through the connections you already have, find people with similar interests, backgrounds or geographical locations, join groups by activity, school or interest, interact through message posts, games, blogs and application sharing, and share your details with the Internet community.

7. **Hi5**: Hi5 shares many similarities with many social network sites; however, it introduces some twists that make it worthwhile for people who love trying out new and interesting online communities. However, it is not one of the popular sites, Hi5 claims around 60 million members from more than 200 countries. One of the site's biggest transformations is the addition of many entertainment options, including games.

8. **Habbo**: The Habbo online community is inhabited by pixelated, cartoon-character alter egos. You can meet others in public rooms (nightclubs, restaurants, shops) and create private rooms for selected friends. Habbo employees heavily moderate the site, catering to its solid teen user base. Most of the users of Habbo are between the age group of 13 – 18 years. Habbo social networks is very popular in places like the United Kingdom, Japan, Sweden, Spain, Italy, Finland and more.

9. **NING**: Ning is the leading online platform for the world's organisers, activists and influencers to create social experiences that inspire action. It helps you create a safe and secure place online for like-minded people. The ability to create your own community makes Ning a great home away from home for organisations and groups looking to fill the social void.

10. **Classmates**: Classmates.com is different from most social networks, in the sense that most of its features are available to premium member. The price for premium members depends on the length of the

agreement – shorter term results in a higher cost per month. Classmates.com is primarily used to reconnect with old classmates. The site features a search engine that lets you view other people who went to the same school you attended.

11. **Tagged**: Tagged is a blend of social networking features that Myspace and Facebook users will find very familiar. Tagged was designed to help users meet lots of new people with similar interests in a short amount of time. This is a free social network that allows you to view your friends' newly uploaded Tagged photo album. Tagged encourages its users to meet strangers based on shared interests, with the idea of growing your network to meet as many people as possible.

12. **myYearbook**: myYearbook, the best place to meet new people and one of the 25 most-trafficked sites. myYearbook has Flash-based games, and the games incorporate Lunch Money. It includes a virtual economy through which people can purchase of gifts which members send to each other. Lunch Money is also donated by members to their favourite charity.

13. **Meetup**: Meetup is an online social networking portal that facilitates offline group meetings in various localities around the world. It makes it easy for anyone to organise a local group or find one of the thousands already meeting up face-to-face. More than 2,000 groups get together in local communities each day.

14. **MyLife**: MyLife (formerly Reunion.com) is a social network service. MyLife can search over 60 social networking sites and other information resources on the web. MyLife searches the web to deliver accurate and timely results. Even in cases when you don't immediately find who you're looking for, MyLife continues searching and provides updates and alerts. MyLife suggests friends and contacts you may know

based on your profile information and existing contacts, including LinkedIn, Facebook and Myspace as well as 50 other sites.

15. **Flixster**: Flixster is a social networking site for movie fans. Users can create their own profiles, invite friends, rate movies and actors, and post movie reviews as well. Flixster.com also operates leading movie applications on Facebook, Myspace, iPhone, Android, and BlackBerry.

16. **myHeritage**: MyHeritage is a family-oriented social network service and genealogy website. It allows members to create their own family websites, share pictures and videos, organise family events, create family trees, and search for ancestors. There are more than 15 million family trees and 91 million photos on the site, and the site is accessible in over 35 languages.

17. **Multiply**: Multiply is a vibrant social shopping destination, but faster and more convenient, where sellers and buyers interact. A user's network is made up of their direct contacts, as well as others who are closely connected to them through their first-degree relationships. Users are also encouraged to specify the nature of their relationship with one another, making it possible to share content based on relationship.

18. **Orkut**: Orkut is a free social networking website where you can create a profile, connect with friends, maintain an online scrapbook and use site features and applications to share your interests and meet others.

19. **Badoo**: Badoo is a multi-lingual social networking website. It is gaining popularity in emerging markets like Russia and Brazil. The site allows users to create profiles, send each other messages, and rate each other's profile pictures at no cost.

20. **Gaia Online**: Gaia Online is a mix of social networking and massive multiplayer online role-playing games. It is a leading online hangout for teens

and young adults, and offers a wide range of features from discussion forums and virtual towns to fully customizable profiles and avatars.

21. **BlackPlanet**: Initially, BlackPlanet was designed as a way for African-American professionals to network. Since then, it's grown and evolved as a site operating under the principles of web 2.0. Members can read other members' blogs, watch music videos, chat with one another, look for new careers and discuss news.

22. **SkyRock**: SkyRock.com is a social networking site that offers its members free web space where they can create a blog, add a profile, and exchange messages with other registered members.

23. **PerfSpot**: PerfSpot provides a web portal for people of any age, gender, or background to share their interests and favourite things on the web. PerfSpot currently publishes its site in 37 different languages, with comprehensive moderator team that screens through up to a million pictures on a daily basis.

24. **Zorpia**: Zorpia.com is a social network that has a large international community. Zorpia's features include profile customization, networking features and an incredibly detailed search.

25. **Netlog**: Netlog (formerly known as Facebox and Bingbox) is a Belgian social networking website specifically targeted at the European youth demographic. On Netlog, you can create your own web page with a blog, pictures, videos, events and much more to share with your friends. Netlog is localized in over 25 languages, to enable users from around the world to access the network.

26. **Tuenti**: Tuenti is an invitation-only private social networking website. It has been referred to as the "Spanish Facebook", by many social network watchers. It is one of the largest social networking sites in Spain. It allows you to set up a profile, upload photos, link

videos and connect and chat with friends. Many other utilities, such as the ability to create events, are also offered. Tuenti is also available as an iPhone App.

27. **Nasza-Klasa.pl**: nasza-klasapl is considered one of the largest and most used social networking sites in Poland. It primarily brings together school's students and alumni. The site is in polish therefore restricting its popularity only to Poland and polish speaking people. Nevertheless, it claims to be the most popular networking site in Poland, and therefore, has found its niche in the competitive social networking space.

28. **IRC-Galleria**: IRC Gallery has been one of the most popular social networking sites for over 10 years is popular within the age group of 18-22. To be able to create an account with this site, at least one of the uploaded images must be accepted by the administrator.

29. **StudiVZ**: StudiVZ is the biggest social networking site in Germany. It is also popular in German-speaking countries like Switzerland and Austria. This site works as a student directory in particular for college and university students in Europe. The site allows students to maintain a personal page that containing their personal information like name, age, study subjects, interests, courses and group memberships.

30. **Xing**: Xing is a professional networking tool. It is popular in countries like Germany, Spain, Portugal, Italy and France. Xing is similar to LinkedIn and claims to have professionals from over 200 countries. It is available in different languages including English, German, Spanish, Portuguese, Italian, French, Dutch, Chinese, Finnish, Swedish, Korean, Japanese, Russian, Polish, Turkish and Hungarian; French and German being the most popularly.

31. **Renren**: Renren is one of the largest social networking sites in China, and caters to people of Chinese origin.

It is very popular among college students. Renren also has a WAP version, which users can access through mobile phones. It features an instant messaging service for its users.

32. **Kaixin001**: Kaixin001 is a popular professional networking tool in China. The target audience for Kaixin's, are typically white-collar middle class who come from a first tier city. This site in China is extremely popular among people who work for multinational companies. Kaixin001 has gained much more popularity since 2009, because social networking sites, such as Myspace, Facebook, Twitter and Youtube were blocked in China.

33. **Hyves.nl**: Hyves, pronounced hives is the largest social network in Netherlands, with many Dutch visitors and members. Hyves Payments and Hyves Games, allows you to play games and pay friends through the social network. Hyves is gaining popularity across Europe.

34. **Millat Facebook**: is a Muslim-oriented social networking website. Originally launched in Pakistan, it has gained popularity in Arab counties as well. This site came into existence after Facebook was banned in Pakisthan. Offers video chat, bulletins, blogs, polls, shout box, and customization of profile page, members can change the page design freely.

35. **Ibibo**: Ibibo stands for iBuild, iBond. It is an Indian social networking site. It is an umbrella site that offers a variety of applications under its social network.

36. **Sonico**: is a free-access social networking website focused on the Latin American audience. You can search and add friends, interact with friends over message, update their own personal profile.

37. **Wer-kennt-wen**: is one of the most popular social networking website in Germany. It is by an invitation-only social networking website, and only for people over 14 years old. Provides the user to write blogs,

chat with friends, and write in their guestbook.

38. **Cyworld**: is a South Korean social network service. It has had a big effect on Korea's Internet culture. Has networks in South Korea, China, and Vietnam and is gaining popularity across Asia and the Pacific Island. Users have access to a profile page, photos, drawings and images uploading, an avatar, neighbourhoods, and clubs.

39. **Mixi**: primarily for Japanese. Offers options to meeting new people, send and receive messages, writing in a diary, read and comment on others' diaries, organise and join communities and invite their friends. The site requires users to own a Japanese cell phone which bars anyone who is not or has not been a resident of Japan.

40. **iWiW**: is a Hungarian social networking web service. Site is an invite-only website, where a user can provide personal information. Users can search for friends using the search tool. Allows users to log in to external websites using their iWiW credentials and is also available for iPone and Android.

This list is not exhaustive and you will probably wish to research and find new social media sites that work for you, and showcase you to best advantage.

Newspapers

National Newspapers

The Daily Telegraph - Daily
The Sunday Telegraph - Sundays
Financial Times - Daily
The Sunday Times - Sunday
The Guardian - Daily
The Observer - Sunday
The Independent - Daily
The Times - Daily
Independent on Sunday - Sunday

'Middle-market' tabloid newspapers

Daily Mail - Daily
Daily Express - Daily
Sunday Express
The Mail on Sunday

Tabloid newspapers

The Sun The Sun on Sunday
Sunday & Daily Mirror
Daily & Sunday Mirror
Sunday & Daily Star
Sunday & The Morning Star
The People Sunday
The Sunday Sport Sunday

Newspapers in England

(Again, this is not an exhaustive list, and should simply be a foundation for your own research.)

Ashford Herald
Aintree & Maghull Champion (weekly free newspaper)
Anfield & Walton Champion (weekly free newspaper)
Berwick Advertiser
Birmingham Mail
Birmingham Post
Bolton News
Bootle Champion (weekly free newspaper)
Bournemouth Daily Echo
The Post, Bristol
Bucks Free Press
Cambridge News
Camden Gazette
Camden New Journal
The Citizen
Cornish Guardian
The Cornishman
Coventry Telegraph
Crosby & Litherland Champion (weekly free newspaper)
Deal and Sandwich Express
Derby Telegraph
Dover Express
Dover Mercury
East Kent Gazette
East Kent Mercury
East Riding Mail
Eastern Daily Press (owned by Archant)
East Anglian Daily Times (owned by Archant)
Express and Echo
Express & Star (Wolverhampton and the Black Country)

Essex Chronicle

Folkestone Herald

Formby Champion (weekly free newspaper)

Gravesend and Dartford Reporter

Hampstead & Highgate Express ("Ham and High")

Hull Daily Mail

Hampshire Chronicle

Hastings Observer

Herne Bay Gazette

Hythe Herald

Isle of Wight County Press

The Journal (Newcastle upon Tyne)

Kent and Sussex Courier

Kent on Saturday

Kent on Sunday

Kent Messenger

Kentish Express

Kentish Gazette

Lancashire Evening Post

Lancashire Telegraph

Leicester Mercury

Lincolnshire Echo

Liverpool Daily Post

Liverpool Echo

London Evening Standard

Lynn News

Manchester Evening News

Medway News

The Mercury (Lichfield, Tamworth and surrounding area)

Mid Sussex Times

Newcastle Evening Chronicle

Newcastle Sunday Sun

Northampton Chronicle & Echo

Northampton Herald & Post

The Northern Echo (North East England)

Nottingham Evening Post

Oldham Chronicle
Ormskirk Advertiser
Ormskirk & West Lancs Champion (weekly free newspaper)
Oxford Mail
Oxford Journal
Oxford Times
Patterdale Chronicle
Peterborough Evening Telegraph
The Press (York)
Reading Chronicle
Romney Marsh Herald
Salford Advertiser
Salford City Reporter
Salisbury Journal
Scunthorpe Telegraph
The Sentinel (Stoke-on-Trent and Staffordshire)
Sevenoaks Chronicle
Sheerness Times Guardian
Sheffield Star
Shropshire Star
Skelmersdale Champion (weekly free newspaper)
Southern Daily Echo
Southport Champion (weekly free newspaper)
Southport Visiter[2]
Southport Reporter
Star Courier Hampshire and Surrey
Stockport Express and Times, Stockport and district
Sunday Independent (South West England)
Sunderland Echo
Tavistock Times Gazette
Teesdale Mercury
The Champion (Southport)[3]
The Argus (Brighton & Hove and Sussex)
The Asian Today (Midlands) (owned by Urban Media)
Yorkshire Post
Watford Observer

The West Briton
Warwickshire Telegraph
Western Daily Press
Western Morning News
Whitstable Gazette
Wigan Observer

Local newspapers
Abingdon
    Abingdon Herald
Accrington
    Accrington Observer
Alnwick
    Northumberland Gazette
Alton
    Alton Herald
Ascot
    Bracknell & Ascot Times
Ashford, Kent
    Ashford Herald
    Kentish Express
    yourashford
    Axminster
    View From Axminster (weekly, free)
    Pulmans Weekly News
Aylesbury
    Bucks Herald
Banbury
    Banbury Cake
    Banbury Guardian
Barnsley
    The Barnsley Chronicle
    The Star[disambiguation needed]
    The Independent
Barrow-in-Furness
    North West Evening Mail

Basildon
    Basildon Yellow Advertiser
Basingstoke
    Basingstoke Gazette
    Basingstoke Observer
Bedfordshire
    Bedfordshire on Sunday
    Times & Citizen
Bicester
    Bicester Advertiser
    Bicester Review
Birmingham
    Birmingham Post (weekly)
    Evening Mail (Daily)
    Forward (Birmingham), formerly the Birmingham Voice
        (published 20 times a year by Birmingham City Council)
    Sports Argus (now just a pull out in the Birmingham Mail)
    Sunday Mercury (Sunday mornings)
Blackpool
    Blackpool Gazette
Bolton
    Bolton News
    Boston, Lincolnshire
    Boston Standard
    Boston Target
Bourne, Lincolnshire
    Bourne Local
Bourne, Lincolnshire/Market Deeping, Lincolnshire & Rutalnd
    Stamford Mercury
Bracknell
    Bracknell News
    Bracknell Standard
    Bracknell Midweek
Bradford
    Telegraph and Argus
Braintree, Essex

Braintree and Witham Times
Bridport (Dorset)
    The Bridport News
Brentwood
    Brentwood Gazette
Bridlington
    Bridlington Free Press
Brighouse
    Brighouse Echo (Weekly, Thursdays)
Brighton
    The Argus (formerly Brighton Evening Argus)
Bristol
    Bristol Evening Post
    Bristol Observer (Weekly, Free)
Bromsgrove
    Bromsgrove Standard
Buckingham
    The Advertiser
Bude (Cornwall)
    Bude & Stratton Post
Burnley
    Burnley Express
Burton-upon-Trent
    Burton Mail
Bury
    Bury Times
    Bury St. Edmunds
    Bury Free Press
Buxton
    Buxton Advertiser
Cambridge
    Cambridge Evening News
Camelford (Cornwall)
    Camelford & Delabole Post
Canterbury
    Canterbury Times

Kentish Gazette
Carlisle
News and Star (Daily except Fridays and Sundays)
Cumberland News (Fridays)
Cumbrian Gazette (weekly; free)
Chesham
Bucks Examiner (weekly)
Chester
Chester Evening Leader
Chester Chronicle (weekly)
Chester and District Standard (weekly; free)
Chester Mail (weekly; free)
Chesterfield
Derbyshire Times
Chew Valley
Chew Valley Gazette
Chichester
Chichester Observer
Chorley
Chorley Citizen (weekly; free)
Chorley Guardian (weekly)
Cirencester
The Wilts & Gloucestershire Standard (weekly established 1837)
Cleobury Mortimer
Teme Valley Times
Coalville
Coalville Times (weekly; also edition in Ashby de la Zouch and Swadlincote)
Cobham
Cobham News & Mail weekly
Colchester
Essex County Standard
Evening Gazette
Congleton
Congleton Chronicle

Coventry
    Coventry Advertiser (monthly; free)
    Coventry Citizen (weekly; free)
    Coventry Telegraph (daily)
    Coventry Observer (weekly; free)
Crawley
    Crawley News
    Crawley Observer
Crewe
    Crewe Chronicle (weekly)
    South Cheshire Mail (weekly, free)
    Crewe Guardian (weekly, free)
Croydon
    Croydon Advertiser (weekly, also editions in NE Surrey)
    Croydon Guardian (weekly, free)
    Croydon Post (weekly, free)
Daventry
    Daventry Express (weekly)
Deal
    Deal and Sandwich Express
    East Kent Mercury
    yourdeal
Derby
    Derby Evening Telegraph
    Derby Express (weekly; free)
    Derby Trader (weekly; free)
Dewsbury
    Dewsbury Reporter
Diss, Norfolk
    Diss Express
Doncaster
    Doncaster Free Press
Driffield
    Driffield Times
    Driffield Post
Droitwich

Droitwich Standard
Dudley
    Dudley News (weekly)
    Express and Star (Dudley version of the Wolverhampton
    newspaper)
Durham
    Darlington & Stockton Times
Teesdale Mercury
    Wear Valley Mercury
Dover
    Dover Express
    Dover Mercury
    yourdover
Durham
    Durham Times
Eastbourne
    Eastbourne Herald
    Eastbourne Gazette
Esher
    Esher News & Mail weekly
Exeter
    Express and Echo
    Flying Post
Exmouth
    Exmouth Journal
Farnborough
    Star Courier
    Farnborough News
Faversham
    Faversham News
    Faversham Times
    yourswale
Fleetwood
    Fleetwood Weekly News
Folkestone
    Folkestone Herald

Kentish Express
yourshepway
Formby
Formby Times
Furness
North-West Evening Mail
Gainsborough
Gainsborough Standard
Garstang
Garstang Courier
Glossop
Glossop Gazette
Glossop Chronicle
Glossop Advertiser
Gloucestershire
Gloucestershire Echo
Gloucester Citizen
The Forester
Stroud Life
Goole
Goole Times
Goole, Howden, Thorne Courier (owned by Johnston Press)
Grantham
Grantham Journal
Gravesend
The Reporter – Formerly The Gravesend Reporter (Archant)
Gravesend Messenger
Grimsby and Northern Lincolnshire
Grimsby Telegraph
Guildford
Surrey Advertiser
Halifax
Halifax Evening Courier
Harlow
Harlow Star
Harlow Scene

The Herald
    The Mercury
Harrogate
    Harrogate Advertiser
Hartlepool
    Hartlepool Mail
Hastings
    Hastings & St. Leonards Observer
Hebden Bridge
    Hebden Bridge Times
    Hemel Hempstead
    Hemel Hempstead Gazette
    Herald Express
Henley-on-Thames
    Henley Standard
Hereford
    Hereford Times
    Herne Bay
    Herne Bay Gazette
    Herne Bay Times
Hertford
    Hertfordshire Mercury
Hertfordshire
    Watford Observer
    Welwyn Hatfield Times
    St Albans Observer
    Herts Advertiser★★
    Hertfordshire Mercury
Heywood
    Heywood Advertiser
Hexham
    Hexham Courant
Holmfirth
    Holme Valley Express
    Holsworthy (Devon)
    Holsworthy Post

Horsham
    The Resident (weekly; free)
Hucknall
    Hucknall and Bulwell Dispatch
Huddersfield
    Huddersfield Daily Examiner
    Colne Valley Chronicle
    Huddersfield & District Chronicle
    Huddersfield Weekly News (free)
Hythe, Kent
    Hythe Herald
    Kentish Express
    yourshepway
Ilkley
    Ilkley Gazette
    Ipswich
    Evening Star (owned by Archant)
Isle of Sheppey
    Sheerness Times Guardian
    Sheppey Gazette
    yourswale
Isle of Wight
    Isle of Wight County Press
    Wight Insight (journal of Isle of Wight Council)
Keighley
    Keighley News
Kendal
    Westmorland Gazette
King's Lynn
    Lynn News & Advertiser (Tues & Fri)
    The Citizen (Weekly, Free)
Kingston upon Hull
    Hull Daily Mail
Lancaster
    Lancaster Guardian
Launceston (Cornwall)

Cornish & Devon Post

Leeds

Leeds Express

Yorkshire Evening Post

Yorkshire Post

Leek

Leek Post and Times

Your Leek Paper

Leicester

Leicester Mercury

Leigh, Greater Manchester

Leigh Reporter

Leigh Journal

Leyland

Leyland Guardian (Weekly)

Lichfield

Lichfield Mercury

Liverpool

Liverpool Daily Post

Liverpool Echo

Mersey Reporter

London – For a more complete listing, see Newspapers in London

Evening Standard (free since late 2009, published by Daily Mail and General Trust plc)

Metro (free, published by Daily Mail and General Trust plc)

London Lite (free, published by Daily Mail and General Trust)

The Londoner, free, published by the Mayor of London

South London Press (Dulwich, Southwark, and Streatham)

Bexley Mercury

Barking & Dagenham Yellow Advertiser

Barking & Dagenham Recorder

Bexley Times

Brent & Wembley Leader

The Press (Barnet and Hendon)

The Wharf (Canary Wharf)

Croydon Advertiser

Croydon Post
Camden New Journal
Camden Gazette
Ealing Gazette
Ealing Leader
Ealing Informer
East London Advertiser
Enfield Advertiser
Enfield Gazette
Fulham & Hammersmith Chronicle
Hackney Gazette
Hammersmith & Kensington Times
Hampstead and Highgate Express
Haringey Advertiser
Harrow Leader
Harrow Informer
Harrow & Wembley Observer
Havering Yellow Advertiser (Romford)
Hornsey & Crouch End Journal
Hounslow Borough Chronicle
Hounslow, Chiswick & Whitton Informer
Ilford Recorder
Ilford & Redbridge Yellow Advertiser
Islington Gazette
Kensington & Chelsea Informer
Kilburn Times
Kingston Informer
Lewisham & Grenwich Mercury
Mitcham, Morden & Wimbledon Post
Muswell Hill Journal
Newham Recorder
Paddington & Westminster Times
Richmond and Twickenham Times
Romford and Havering Post
Staines Informer
Staines Leader

Stratford & Newham Express
Streatham, Clapham & West Norwood Post
Surrey Herald
Surrey Mirror Advertiser
Sutton & Epsom Post
Tottenham, Wood Green and Edmonton Journal
Uxbridge Gazette
Uxbridge & Hillingdon Leader
Wanstead and Woodford Guardian
Wembley & Kingsbury Times
Willesden & Brent Times
Loughborough
Loughborough Echo
Loughborough Mail
Loughborough Trader Xtra
Loughton
Loughton Guardian (part of the Newsquest group)
Ludlow
Teme Valley Times
Luton
Herald and Post
Luton on Sunday
Lyme Regis
View From Lyme Regis (weekly, free)
Macclesfield
The Macclesfield Express (weekly, owned by M.E.N)
Maidstone
Kent Messenger
yourmaidstone
Malton
Malton Gazette & Herald (weekly)
Manchester
Manchester Evening News
Mansfield
Chad (Chronicle Advertiser)
Market Drayton

Market Drayton Advertiser
Market Harborough
Harborough Mail
Market Rasen
Market Rasen Mail
Medway
Medway News
Medway Messenger
Medway Standard
yourmedway
Middlesbrough
Evening Gazette
Middleton, Greater Manchester
Middleton Guardian
Milton Keynes
Milton Keynes Citizen
MK News
Minehead
West Somerset Free Press
Molesey
Molesey News & Mail weekly
Newbury
Newbury Weekly News
Newcastle upon Tyne
Evening Chronicle
The Journal
Metro (free, published by Daily Mail and General Trust)
Sunday Sun
Chronicle Extra (free weekly Newspaper for all of Newcastle)
New Romney
Kentish Express
Romney Marsh Herald
yourshepway
Newtownabbey
Newtownabbey Times
Northampton

Northampton Chronicle & Echo
Northampton Mercury
Northwich
Northwich Guardian
North Yorkshire
North Yorkshire News (free)
The Advertiser (free)
Norwich
Norwich Evening News (daily)
The Advertiser (Archant) (weekly, free)
Nottinghamshire
Nottingham Evening Post
Newark Advertiser
Worksop Guardian
Oldham
Oldham Advertiser
Oldham Evening Chronicle
Ormskirk
Ormskirk and West Lancashire Advertiser
Ormskirk and West Lancashire Champion
Oxford
Oxford Times
Oxford Mail
Oxford Star
Penrith
Cumberland and Westmorland Herald (Saturdays)
Peterborough
Peterborough Evening Telegraph (daily, part of East Midlands
Newspapers, owned by Johnston Press)
Peterlee
Peterlee Star (weekly)
Pickering
Pickering Gazette & Herald (weekly)
Plymouth
Western Morning News
Plymouth Evening Herald

Portsmouth
    The News
    Sports Mail (weekly, football)
Prestwich
    Prestwich and Whitefield Guide
Reading
    Reading Chronicle
    Reading Evening Post
Retford
    Retford Times
    Retford Trader and Guardian
Ripon
    Ripon Gazette
Rochdale
    Rochdale Observer
Romford
    Romford Recorder
Romsey
    Romsey Advertiser
Rotherham
    Rotherham Advertiser
Royston
    Royston Crow
Rugby
    Rugby Observer (weekly, free)
    Rugby Advertiser (weekly)
St. Helens
    St. Helens Reporter
Salford
    Salford Advertiser
Sandwich
    Deal and Sandwich Express
    East Kent Mercury
    yoursandwich
Scarborough
    Scarborough Evening News

Scarborough Mercury later The Mercury (weekly)
Scunthorpe
    Scunthorpe Telegraph
Selby
    Selby Post
    Selby Times
    Selby Star
Seaford, East Sussex
    Seaford Gazette
Sevenoaks
    Sevenoaks Chronicle
    Sheffield
    Sheffield Star
Stamford and Rutland
    Stamford Mercury
    Sheffield Telegraph
Shrewsbury
    Shrewsbury Chronicle
Sittingbourne
    East Kent Gazette
Skipton
    Craven Herald & Pioneer
Slough
    Slough Express
Sleaford
    Sleaford Target
    Sleaford Standard
Southend
    The Evening Echo
Southport
    Southport Visiter
    Southport Champion
    Southport Reporter
South Tyneside
    Shields Gazette (the oldest provincial evening newspaper in
    the United Kingdom)

Stafford
  Stafford & Stone Chronicle
Stockport
  Stockport Express
  Stoke-on-Trent
  The Sentinel
Sunderland
  Sunderland Echo
Sutton Coldfield
  Sutton Coldfield Observer
Stroud
  Stroud News and Journal
Swindon
  Swindon Advertiser
  Swindon Star
  Tameside (metropolitan borough of Greater Manchester)
  Tameside Advertiser
  Tameside Reporter
Tamworth
  Tamworth Herald
Taunton
  The Somerset County Gazette (weekly, focus on Taunton)
  The Taunton Times (weekly, free)
Tenbury Wells
  Teme Valley Times
Tenterden
  Kentish Express
  yourashford
  Isle of Thanet
  Isle of Thanet Gazette
  Thanet Adscene
  Thanet Extra
  Thanet Times
  yourthanet
Todmorden
  Todmorden News

Torbay (and South Devon)
Herald Express
Vale of Belvoir
The Village Voice (monthly, free)
Melton Times
Wakefield
Wakefield Express
Wakefield Express Extra (weekly, free)
Walton
Walton News & Mail weekly
Warminster
Warminster Journal
Warrington
Warrington Guardian
Wetherby
Wetherby News
Weybridge
Weybridge News & Mail weekly
Whitby
Whitby Gazette (weekly)
Whitchurch, Shropshire
Whitchurch Herald
Whitstable
Whitstable Gazette
Whitstable Times
Widnes
Widnes World (weekly)
Widnes Weekly News (weekly)
Wigan
Wigan Evening Post
Wigan Observer
Wigan Reporter
Wiltshire
Wiltshire Times
Gazette and Herald
Winchester

Winchester Today
Wirral
    Wirral Globe
    Wirral News (editions for Wallasey, Birkenhead, Hoylake & West Kirby, Heswall, Bromborough etc.)
Wokingham
    Wokingham Times
Wolverhampton
    Express and Star (covering Black Country, largest-selling regional evening newspaper in the UK)
Worcestershire
    Kidderminster Shuttle (weekly, free)
Worcester
    Worcester News (part of the Newsquest group)
    Berrow's Worcester Journal (part of the Newsquest group)
Worksop
    Worksop Guardian
    Worksop Trader
Yeovil
    Western Gazette
York
    York Press

Find out more about job hunting, Chris Gillmore
and Chris' recruitment companies at:

Accord Appointments
www.accordappointments.co.uk

Paragons Personnel
www.paragons.co.uk

Lightning Source UK Ltd.
Milton Keynes UK
UKOW04f1247240914

239094UK00012B/126/P